S0-CPE-119

Any Number Can Play

Also by George Sullivan

CENTER

PITCHER

QUARTERBACK

RUN, RUN FAST!

Any Number Can Play

by George Sullivan

illustrated by John Caldwell

Thomas Y. Crowell   New York

Any Number Can Play
Text copyright © 1990 by George Sullivan
Illustrations copyright © 1990 by John Caldwell
Printed in the U.S.A. All rights reserved.
Typography by Patricia Tobin
10 9 8 7 6 5 4 3 2 1
First Edition

Library of Congress Cataloging-in-Publication Data
Sullivan, George, 1927–
    Any number can play / by George Sullivan :
illustrated by John Caldwell.
        p.   cm.
    Summary: Includes anecdotes recounting
the history and lore associated with the
numbers on athletes' uniforms.
    ISBN 0-690-04812-2 : $. — ISBN 0-690-04814-9 (lib. bdg.) :
$
    1. Uniforms, Sports—History—Juvenile literature. 2. Uniforms,
Sports—Anecdotes—Juvenile literature. [1. Sports—History.
2. Sports—Miscellaneous.]   I. Caldwell, John, 1946–   ill.
II. Title.
GV749.U53 1990   89-35501
796'.028—dc20   CIP
                                                       AC

Acknowledgments

Many people helped in providing information used in this book. Special thanks are due Howard Talbot and Bill Guilfoyle, Baseball Hall of Fame; Rich Levin, Office of the Baseball Commissioner; Joe Horrigan, Pro Football Hall of Fame; Kenny Albert, National Hockey League; and Barbara and John Devaney, Don Wigal and Tim Sullivan.

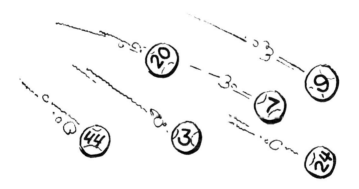

Any Number Can Play

Introduction

On the Friday after Thanksgiving Day in 1984, two of college football's most exciting teams, the University of Miami and Boston College, faced one another in Miami's Orange Bowl. Boston College, thanks mostly to the strong right arm of quarterback Doug Flutie, scored one touchdown after another during the long, rain-soaked afternoon.

But Miami kept fighting back. As the game entered its final minutes, Miami spurted into the lead, 45–41.

When Boston College took over the ball for the last time, only 28 seconds remained. There were 80 yards to go for a touchdown.

Flutie passed for 19 yards. Another pass gained 10 yards.

Flutie glanced at the scoreboard—6 seconds remained.

Once more Flutie took the snap and sprinted back to throw. Miami defenders poured in. Flutie circled to his right, scanning the Miami end zone 65 yards away.

Flutie planted his right foot and fired. The ball sailed through the mist.

Gerald Phelan, Flutie's favorite receiver, had outraced the man covering him. His left foot was on the goal line when the ball nestled into his arms. *Touchdown*. Boston College had won, 47–45. The scoreboard clock read: "00.0."

That miracle pass, watched by millions on television, made twenty-two-year-old Doug Flutie an instant celebrity. In the months that followed, football jerseys with Flutie's No. 22 on the back sold like hotcakes. "If I had a nickel for every kid I saw wearing a 22 Flutie jersey," said a Boston College official, "I'd be a millionaire."

It happens all the time. When pitcher Dwight Gooden was throwing bullets for the New York Mets, kids in New York started wearing No. 16. Every young basketball player knows that Earvin "Magic" Johnson of the Lakers wears No. 32 and that Michael Jordan of the Chicago Bulls is No. 23.

Uniform numbers are a direct link between a fan and his or her hero. There's something personal and satisfying about wearing a jersey that bears your idol's number.

Of course, to the players themselves, numbers are often a very serious matter. Sometimes a player becomes attached to a certain number in high school or even earlier. The player may feel that the number has an effect on how he or she performs. It's something like wearing lucky shoes or eating right before a game.

It's no wonder then that a player will try to keep the same number throughout his or her career. First baseman Steve Garvey, in the fourteen years he spent with the Los Angeles Dodgers, always wore No. 6. When Garvey left the Dodgers to sign with the San Diego Padres in 1983, Tim Flannery was wearing No. 6. So Garvey bought Flannery a new suit to get him to give up his number.

This book takes a lighthearted look at uniform numbers. While it is meant to inform you, explaining how the use of numbers began and examining the strict numbering systems that some sports follow, the book is mostly meant to entertain. In other words, you get some fun along with the facts. Enjoy!

Dealing in Fractions

One of the wackiest stunts in baseball history took place on August 19, 1951. The St. Louis Browns faced the Detroit Tigers in a double-header at Sportsman's Park in St. Louis. In the first inning of the second game, manager Zack Taylor sent Eddie Gaedel up to bat for right-fielder Frank Saucier.

There were about 18,000 fans in the stands, and they could hardly believe their eyes. Gaedel was smaller than the smallest Little Leaguer. He stood 3 feet 7—the only midget ever to appear in a major league baseball game.

The idea of having a midget take a turn at bat had been dreamed up by Bill Veeck, owner of the Browns. Veeck was always staging one kind of an event or another to entertain the fans.

He had been planning the stunt for several weeks. As a uniform for Gaedel, Veeck borrowed the uniform that belonged to the seven-year-old son of the club's vice president. Veeck bought a toy bat for Gaedel to use, and agreed to pay him one hundred dollars for his appearance.

In his turn at bat, Gaedel, a right-handed hitter, spread his feet wide apart, cocked his little bat, and eyed the pitcher. He was very serious. The pitcher was unable to put the ball into Gaedel's tiny strike zone, and so he walked on four straight pitches. Jim Delsing was sent in to run for him.

As Gaedel trotted across the field to the St. Louis dugout, the crowd cheered. Eddie waved his cap and grinned.

So ended the baseball career of Eddie Gaedel, the smallest player in baseball history. On his back that day he wore, fittingly, the smallest uniform number in baseball history: 1/8.

Missed Opportunity

Duffy Daugherty, former football coach at Michigan State University, once had a running back named James Bond. Daugherty thought it would be a cute idea to have the player wear No. 007. He asked the National Collegiate Athletic Association (NCAA), the governing body of college sports, for permission to have him do so. The NCAA said no. Too bad for James Bond. With 007 on his back, he surely would have become one of the most famous college players of all time.

Favored Treatment

In professional ice hockey, it's traditional for the goalie to wear No. 1. During the 1988–89 season, for example, more than half of all National Hockey League (NHL) teams followed the custom. The reason goalies wear No. 1 goes back to an earlier period in the sport, to the 1930s and 40s.

In those days, teams traveled from one city to another by train. On overnight trips, players slept in railroad-car berths. These were narrow, built-in platform beds, one stacked above the other. Since a person could sleep better in the bottommost berth, that's what every player wanted.

But there weren't enough lower berths for everyone. Someone came up with the idea of assigning them according to uniform numbers. No. 1 would be given first choice as to sleeping accommodations, No. 2 second choice, etc. This system assured that the senior members of the team, those who traditionally wore the lowest numbers, would get the bottom bunks.

Playing goalie in those days was about the

same as it is today: rough and rugged. Goalies were usually exhausted after games. It was taken for granted that the team's goalie was more deserving of a bottom bunk than any other player. So teams began assigning goalies the lowest number of all. Even though teams now travel by plane, the No. 1 tradition has lasted to this day.

A Look Back

The game of baseball, which has been traced all the way back to the 1840s, was played for almost a century before teams got around to putting numbers on players' backs on a regular basis. The New York Yankees, who wore numbers for the first time in 1929, are usually cited as the team that introduced their use.

Numbering players, however, was tried as early as 1888, when the Cincinnati Reds wore numbers on their sleeves. But the idea failed to catch on. The Cleveland Indians experimented with sleeve numbers in 1916, and the St. Louis Cardinals tried them in 1924. In each case, the numbers lasted for only the season.

When the Yankees put numbers on the backs of players in 1929, the club had each man's number correspond to his position in the batting order. Babe Ruth batted third and Lou Gehrig was the cleanup hitter for the 1929 Yankees. That's how Ruth wound up with No. 3 and Gehrig with No. 4. These came to rank as two of the most famous numbers in baseball history.

Here's the complete lineup:

No. 1   Earl Combs, *center field*
No. 2   Mark Koenig, *third base*
No. 3   Babe Ruth, *right field*
No. 4   Lou Gehrig, *first base*
No. 5   Bob Meusel, *left field*
No. 6   Tony Lazzeri, *second base*
No. 7   Leo Durocher, *shortstop*
No. 8   Nig Grabowski, *catcher*

The second-string catcher was assigned No. 9. Pitchers were given Nos. 10 through 19, and nonregular players had to wear Nos. 20 and beyond.

Opening Day for the Yankees in 1929 was set for Tuesday, April 16, with the Boston Red Sox furnishing the opposition, but the game was canceled by rain. The teams were rained out the next day, too. Finally, on Thursday, April 18, the teams got a chance to play, although the day was cold and gray. The Yanks won, 7–3, with Ruth and Gehrig hitting homers.

There was no team in baseball better than the Yankees during this time. They had captured three straight American League pennants and won the World Series in 1927 and 1928. "When the Bronx Bombers sneezed in those days," *Sports Illustrated* once noted, "the rest of the league said, 'Bless you.' " Just about every other team was numbering its players by 1930.

Two for the Money

At the Indianapolis 500, the most famous auto race in the world, put your money on No. 2. In the seventy-three runnings of the race (through 1989), No. 2 won eight times, more than any other number. No. 1 and No. 3 were close, each with seven wins. No. 14 had five victories.

The numbers to avoid are 10, 11, 13, 18 and 19 and anything in the 50s. They've never won.

Being Different

When Chris Mullin, a basketball standout at St. John's University during the early 1980s, joined the Golden State Warriors of the National Basketball Association (NBA) in 1985, he picked uniform No. 17. Why? Because his boyhood hero, John Havlicek of the Boston Celtics, had worn No. 17.

That's how many players choose their uniform numbers. It's a number that once belonged to someone they admired.

But there are plenty of other reasons for choosing a certain number. Consider the following:

Carlos May, an outfielder with the Chicago White Sox, picked No. 17 because he was born on May 17 (1948). May liked the idea of wearing his birthday on his back.

Sid Fernandez, ace left-hander of the New York Mets, is from Hawaii. You might have been able to figure that out from the number he chose, No. 50. To Fernandez, it was a tribute to Hawaii, the fiftieth state.

Sam Perkins of the Dallas Mavericks of the National Basketball Association chose No. 41

because it happened to be his sleeve length in inches.

Pitcher Jerry Reuss of the Chicago White Sox was inspired to wear No. 41 by a highway sign he once saw. "There was something about it that just appealed to me," he said.

Frank Quilici, an infielder for the Minnesota Twins, wore No. 7 because he felt it was lucky. Quilici was released by the Twins in 1971, then later rehired as a coach. He asked for his No. 7. It was gone; someone else was wearing it. Quilici then went to 43 because the digits added up to 7.

Mike Adamle, a running back for the Kansas City Chiefs and New York Jets during the 1970s, stood 5 feet 9 and weighed 188 pounds. That's not very big for a pro football running back. Realizing this, Adamle wore No. 1. He said it made him look taller.

Trivia Question I

Hank Aaron made No. 44 famous for all time. But in 1954, his first year in the major leagues, Aaron did not wear No. 44. What was Aaron's number as a rookie?

Answer: see page 119

Moneymaker

In 1908, well before uniform numbers came into general use in college football, the University of Pittsburgh began numbering its backfield players—the quarterback, fullback and two halfbacks. According to *The History of American Football*, this was the work of Karl Davis, the team's publicity manager. Davis had been given the rights to print and sell programs for Pitt games.

Davis had a gimmick. He made sure the players wore different jerseys for each game. That meant that a new program had to be purchased each week. Fortunately for the sports fans who might prefer to spend their money on hot dogs, peanuts or something else, Davis' idea never caught on.

Jokester

Bill Lee, who pitched for the Boston Red Sox and Montreal Expos, was known more for his zaniness than his fastball or curve. He once went to the mound wearing a coonskin cap. Another time it was a gas mask.

Lee, whose fourteen-year career ended in 1982, wore No. 37. But that number was only two-thirds of the number he really wanted— 337. It was the perfect number for him. You see, he was aware that when you turn 337 upside down, it spells out L-E-E.

A Helmetful of Numbers

Jersey numbers in college football were first used around the turn of the century. But teams followed no standard policy. Some teams wore numbers; others didn't bother. And on still other teams, only the captain had a number. It appeared on the front of his jersey. It was usually 1 or 0.

According to Dr. L. H. Baker, writing in *Football Facts & Figures*, the first time two teams with numbered jerseys lined up against one another was in 1913. The teams were the University of Wisconsin and the University of Chicago.

After that, the use of numbers spread fast. When the National Football League (NFL) set up shop in the early 1920s, virtually every team numbered its players. One reason was money. The numbers were printed in programs that were sold to fans. Teams struggled to survive in those days. Programs represented a source of much-needed income.

A pro player usually wore whatever jersey the team's equipment manager happened to toss him. If a player changed teams, he usually got a different number. And players' numbers usually differed from one season to the next, even if they stayed with the same team.

The great Jim Thorpe, for instance, who played halfback for several teams in pro football's earliest days, is known to have worn at least three different numbers: 1, 3 and 21.

Steve Owen, who entered pro football in the 1930s as a lineman and coach for the New York Giants, is usually identified with No. 55. But

Owen also wore 9, 36 and 44 during his career.

Football's number champion is Johnny "Blood" McNally, a halfback and one of football's original free spirits. McNally played for such teams as the Milwaukee Badgers, Duluth Eskimos, Pottsville Maroons and Green Bay Packers—and some others. As he moved from one club to the next, he kept wearing different numbers, at least seven of them—10, 14, 15, 20, 24, 55 and 57. Four numbers more and McNally would have had enough for an entire team.

Hexed

Ralph Branca, a pitcher for the Brooklyn Dodgers in the 1940s and early 1950s, is the player most closely linked to No. 13 and the bad luck it supposedly bestows. "I got No. 13 when I was a rookie in 1944," Branca once recalled. "The clubhouse man said it was the only uniform my size, but that if I was superstitious I could change it. I decided to keep it. I thought it might be lucky."

The number was no factor in Branca's early years with the team. In 1947, he won 21 games. "Not many pitchers ever do that," he once noted.

Branca became forever known for wearing No. 13 in 1951. By mid-August that year, the Dodgers were leading the second-place New York Giants by $13\frac{1}{2}$ games in the National League pennant race. Then the Giants began chipping away at the big Dodger lead. In one of the most stunning comebacks in baseball history, the Giants tied the Dodgers on the final day of the season. A three-game playoff resulted. The Giants won the first game, the Dodgers the second.

In the bottom of the ninth inning of the deciding game, with the Dodgers leading 4–2, Branca was called in from the bullpen to replace the starting pitcher. Bobby Thomson was the batter. Two men were on base. There was one out. Branca's first pitch was a strike. On the next, a fastball, Thomson lofted a high fly into left field that plopped into the stands for a home run. The Giants had won the pennant. Their joyous fans streamed out onto the field.

Branca turned and started for the clubhouse, his shoulders slumped. Never had bad fortune struck a baseball player so swiftly and so surely. Branca, with his No. 13, had tempted fate and lost.

When Branca reported to training camp in the spring of 1952, a No. 12 jersey was waiting for him. The club had put his No. 13 into storage.

With Due Respect

Humble, according to the dictionary, means being modest, not proud. Bill Walton, 6 feet 11, from La Mesa, California, an exceptional center in both college and professional basketball, was humble in picking out his uniform numbers.

At UCLA in the early 1970s, Walton wore No. 32. The reason: Lew Alcindor, a three-time All-America selection with the Bruins, had worn No. 33. Walton explained that he did not feel he was quite the equal of Mr. Alcindor (who, as Kareem Abdul-Jabbar, went on to become a pro superstar with the Los Angeles Lakers), and thus his number should be one digit less than Alcindor's.

Wearing No. 32, Walton led UCLA to the NCAA title in 1972 and 1973. Following college, Walton embarked on a pro career with the Portland Trail Blazers, where he continued to wear No. 32.

The Boston Celtics acquired Walton in 1985. Again he wanted to wear No. 32, but it was owned by Kevin McHale. In picking out a new number, Walton used the same reasoning he

had used earlier. He realized that in joining the Celtics he was following in the footsteps of the great Bill Russell, who wore No. 6. Walton's choice was—you guessed it—No. 5.

Setting a Limit

In what major American sport are players prohibited from wearing these numbers?

It's basketball. Uniform numbers in college and professional basketball cannot use any digit higher than 5. Numbers 6, 7, 8 and 9 are rarer than five-feet tall All-Stars.

It's not hard to understand why such a rule is in effect. It has to do with the way in which basketball officials call fouls. When a foul occurs, the referee designates the offender's number by using his or her fingers. For example, if the offender's number is 25, the referee holds up two fingers on the left hand and five fingers on the right. This means "two five" to the scorers.

As you can imagine, any numeral larger than a five would disrupt communications between the officials and the scorers.

In professional basketball, there is no official rule saying that uniform numbers cannot include digits greater than 5. "It's a tradition we follow," says a spokesperson for the National Basketball Association. "Theoretically, a player could wear any number."

Despite the absence of an official rule, no professional player in recent years has worn a 6, 7, 8 or 9. The most notable exception was George Mikan of the Minneapolis Lakers, a dominant figure in pro basketball's early years. Mikan, who retired in 1956, wore No. 99.

It has happened before. Undoubtedly it will happen again.

Presidential Numbers

Former U.S. presidents Dwight D. Eisenhower, Richard Nixon, Gerald Ford and Ronald Reagan all played college football. What numbers did they wear?

Ronald Reagan, a good athlete, earned letters in swimming and track at Eureka College in Eureka, Illinois, in the 1930s. He was a guard on the football team. His football coach at Eureka once described him as a dedicated player who worked hard. "He was a plugger," the coach said. No. 80 was Reagan's jersey number.

Reagan is also linked to football for his portrayal of George Gipp in the movie *Knute Rockne—All American*. Rockne was a famous coach at the University of Notre Dame, and Gipp was a legendary player. Gipp first played for Notre Dame in 1916. That was before Notre Dame football players wore numbers. So Reagan was numberless in the movie.

Gerald Ford, the thirty-eighth president, was perhaps the best athlete of all recent White House occupants. He skied and was a skilled swimmer. At the University of Michigan, Ford was the

center and captain of the football team. He wore No. 48.

Richard Nixon, who preceded Ford in the White House, tried out for the football team when he was a student at Whittier College in Whittier, California. But he got to play only on the freshman squad. For the rest of his college career, Nixon was a bench sitter. Nixon wore jersey No. 12.

Dwight D. Eisenhower, like Ford a gifted athlete, played left halfback for the U.S. Military Academy at West Point. His athletic career was cut short when he damaged his knee while tackling the great Jim Thorpe. That was in 1912. Football jerseys at West Point didn't begin to have numbers until 1916. So Eisenhower never wore a number.

Removing a Hex

Louis Schneider, a twenty-three-year-old motorcycle cop, arrived at the Indianapolis Speedway in 1931 with an 8-cylinder blue-and-red Barnes Speed Fast Special, eager to compete against the better-known cars with their famous drivers. Speedway officials took one look at Schneider's automobile and were filled with alarm. It had a huge No. 13 on each side of the hood. A 13 at Indianapolis or any other race track is about as welcome as an oil slick on a sharp turn. Officials made Schneider paint over the 13. Schneider went on to win the race that year. Maybe not having that No. 13 helped.

Lucky Day

It was hailed as the "luckiest day of the century." It was the seventh day of the seventh month of the seventy-seventh year. It was July 7, 1977, or 7/7/77.

The Taft Hotel at 777 Seventh Avenue in New York City celebrated with a party at which prizes were awarded every seven minutes. At the Landmark Hotel in Las Vegas, a buffet lunch was offered for 77 cents, and two tickets to a musical review cost $7.77. In Maryland, lottery officials were stunned by the thousands of people who wanted to play No. 777. They had to stop taking bets on it. If they hadn't and the number had happened to win, it would have put the lottery out of business.

In major league baseball on the "luckiest day of the century," five players wearing No. 7 jerseys saw action. They were:

> Rick Burleson, *Boston Red Sox*
> Dave Chalk, *California Angels*
> Ed Kranepool, *New York Mets*
> Bobby Murcer, *Chicago Cubs*
> Steve Yeager, *Los Angeles Dodgers*

Did any or all of them hit game-winning home runs that day? Were they dazzling in the field?

Not at all. While three of the players—Burleson, Murcer and Yeager—saw their teams win, none of the five had an outstanding day. Yeager was the batting star of the five, smacking a two-run homer that helped the Dodgers down the Astros 7–4. But it was Yeager's only hit in four trips to the plate.

Overall, the five players had three hits in a total of seventeen at bats. That figures out to a .176 average.

What does this mean? One thing it means is while it's nice to wear a lucky number, you can't depend on it for results. You'd better have talent, too.

40

Luck of the Draw

On October 18, 1924, Harold "Red" Grange of the University of Illinois scored 4 touchdowns against Michigan. And he did it in the first 12 minutes of the game. Grange wore No. 77 that day. For what he did that afternoon and for all he accomplished as a running back in the years that followed, the number became forever identified with Grange. He was even sometimes referred to as "ol' 77."

John Underwood of *Sports Illustrated* once asked Grange how he happened to get his famous number. Grange recalled the first practice he attended. "The guy in front of me got No. 76," Grange said. "The guy in back of me got 78."

Being Original

When Steve Bagarus, a running back from Notre Dame, signed a contract with the Washington Redskins in 1945, he used his imagination in choosing his number. He asked for and got No. 00, explaining, "I want the players on the other team to say 'Oh Oh' when I come into the game."

Bagarus stood 6 feet and weighed 173 pounds, not very big by today's standards. He retired after the 1948 season. The record book shows that in his short stay in the pro game he carried the ball 98 times for 343 yards, so-so statistics for the first "oh-oh" player.

The First

A big, quiet and very determined man, Lou Gehrig began playing first base regularly for the New York Yankees on June 1, 1925. His batting feats have seldom been equaled. He hit 40 or more home runs five times. He twice led the American League with 49 homers. The 184 runs he batted in in 1931 is still a league record. He led the league in batting in 1934 with a .363 average, and he had a lifetime average of .340.

Year in, year out, Gehrig was at first base for the Yankees despite the assorted aches and pains ball players are subject to. He did not take himself out of the lineup until May 2, 1939. He had become too ill to play, because of a crippling disease that was to claim his life two years later. Between 1925 and 1939, Gehrig played in 2,130 consecutive games, an iron-man streak that is not likely to be repeated.

On July 4, 1939, soon after he had dropped from the lineup, the Yankees held "Lou Gehrig Day" at Yankee Stadium, and his No. 4 uniform was retired. Gehrig, in his speech of appreciation, said he was the luckiest man alive.

The ceremony at Yankee Stadium marked the first time a club had ever taken a number out of use to honor a player. Other baseball teams and then teams in other sports soon began to adopt the practice.

Right Size

Billy Martin, who was hired (and fired) several times as manager of the New York Yankees, had his No. 1 retired by the team in 1986. A second baseman for the Yankees during the 1950s, Martin was named the Most Valuable Player (MVP) of the 1953 World Series, perhaps his most noted achievement. His lifetime batting average was a mere .257. At the ceremony in which his number was retired, Martin declared that he was the "proudest" Yankee ever to wear pinstripes.

Up until the time he was drafted into the military service in 1954, the smallish Martin had always worn No. 12. While Martin was in the service, uniform No. 1 became available. "Pete Sheehy [the Yankee clubhouse manager at the time] saved it for me," Martin once explained. "He said my back wasn't big enough for two numbers."

Trivia Question II

Professional soccer in the United States can claim only one memorable number. It is No. 10, worn during the 1970s by a player for the Cosmos of the North American Soccer League. Who was that player?

Answer: see page 119

Rare Tribute

Among pro football running backs, No. 32 is held in the highest esteem. The number first became famous when worn by Hall of Famer Jim Brown, who set more than a dozen National Football League rushing records as a member of the Cleveland Browns during the late 1950s and early 1960s. Many people say that Brown is the best running back of all time.

Many of Brown's records were eventually wiped out by O. J. Simpson, who signed on with the San Francisco 49ers in 1978 after an exceptional career with the Buffalo Bills. Simpson, like Brown, wore No. 32.

Other running backs, perhaps hoping to run with the success of either Brown or Simpson, adopted No. 32. These included Franco Harris of the Pittsburgh Steelers, an outstanding performer for more than a decade beginning in 1972, and Ottis Anderson of the St. Louis Cardinals, the NFL's Rookie of the Year in 1979 and a fearsome runner in the years that followed.

More recently, running backs who have piled

more glory upon No. 32 have included Marcus Allen of the Los Angeles Raiders, the NFL's leading rusher in 1985; Craig James, who helped to power the New England Patriots to the Super Bowl in 1985; and James Wilder of the Tampa Bay Buccaneers, not only the team's leading rusher but also its best pass receiver.

No. 32 was singled out in an unusual way during the 1985–86 television season. On one episode of *The Cosby Show* Rudy Huxtable, the

youngest of the Huxtable daughters, joined a neighborhood football team made up of boys and girls her own age.

Rudy, a running back, was an enormous success in the very first game she played, scoring one touchdown after another, four of them in all. The Huxtable family cheered wildly from the sidelines. In the tradition of Jim Brown, O. J. Simpson and many others, Rudy wore No. 32.

Four-Wheeled Numbers

Auto racing has its numbers, too, the big, bold numbers that are painted on the sides of each driver's car. To auto-racing fans, some of these numbers are just as well known as Babe Ruth's No. 3 or Hank Aaron's No. 44.

The list includes:

No. 9   Bill Elliott, *the first driver to win $2 million in a single season.*

No. 11   Darrell Waltrip, *the winningest driver of the 1980s.*

No. 14   A. J. Foyt, *the only four-time winner of the Indianapolis 500.*

No. 22   Bobby Allison, *a favorite of the fans for more than twenty years.*

No. 28   Cale Yarborough, *winner of more than five hundred races and approximately $5 million in prize money.*

No. 43   Richard Petty, *king of the stock-car drivers.*

Following a Formula

When Danny Buggs, a college football player at West Virginia University, arrived at the training camp of the New York Giants in the summer of 1975, he asked for jersey No. 8. "You can't wear No. 8," he was told. "You're a wide receiver. You have to wear a number in the 80s."

Buggs was given No. 86, which didn't make him happy. "No. 8 means a lot to me," he said. "I wore it in college. Our other wide receiver wore No. 9. It's psychological or something. I don't know. I feel lighter in 8; I feel faster."

Danny Buggs was no exception. Hundreds of pro football players wear jersey numbers that have no particular meaning for them. That's because of the National Football League's number-by-position policy. It states that players' jerseys must be numbered as follows:

Quarterbacks and kickers: 1 through 19
Running backs and defensive backs: 20 through 49
Centers and linebackers: 50 through 59
All linemen: 60 through 79
Wide receivers and tight ends: 80 through 89

Numbering by position, which the NFL introduced in 1972, was once tried by baseball's National League. Managers, coaches and catchers were to wear numbers from 1 to 9; infielders, 10 to 19; outfielders, 20 to 29, etc. But the players protested. They said they liked the numbers they had and did not want to give them up. Baseball abandoned the plan. Danny Buggs should have been a baseball player.

College Code

The National Collegiate Athletic Association "strongly recommends" that football jerseys be numbered from 1 through 99 according to this diagram:

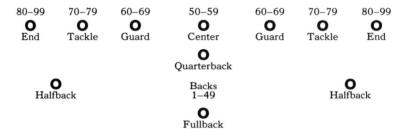

80–99	70–79	60–69	50–59	60–69	70–79	80–99
O	**O**	**O**	**O**	**O**	**O**	**O**
End	Tackle	Guard	Center	Guard	Tackle	End

O
Quarterback

O   Backs   **O**
Halfback   1–49   Halfback
O
Fullback

Two other NCAA rules are meant to avoid number trickery. Players are not permitted to change numbers during a game. Nor are players on the same team permitted to wear the same number at the same time on the same down. Just imagine the confusion that could cause!

Half a Number
Is Better Than None

Quarterback Doug Flutie made No. 22 popular from coast to coast while playing for Boston College (as noted earlier in this book). But when Flutie joined the Chicago Bears in 1986, he had to abide by the National Football League rule that limited quarterbacks to Nos. 1 through 19. Flutie made the best of it; he took No. 2.

Honored Numbers

Since July 4, 1939, when the New York Yankees retired Lou Gehrig's No. 4 in the very first ceremony of its type, about eighty great baseball players have seen their numbers taken out of use.

No. 4 is the number that major league teams have honored the most often. Seven players have seen their No. 4s pass into retirement. They are:

> Luke Appling, *Chicago White Sox*
> Joe Cronin, *Boston Red Sox*
> Lou Gehrig, *New York Yankees*
> Ralph Kiner, *Pittsburgh Pirates*
> Mel Ott, *San Francisco Giants*
> Duke Snider, *Los Angeles Dodgers*
> Earl Weaver, *Baltimore Orioles*

Every number from 1 through 21 has been honored at least once, except Nos. 12 and 13.

The New York Yankees have retired twelve numbers (and honored thirteen individuals), more than any other team. They are:

> No. 1   Billy Martin
> No. 3   Babe Ruth

No. 4   Lou Gehrig
No. 5   Joe DiMaggio
No. 7   Mickey Mantle
No. 8   Yogi Berra, Bill Dickey
No. 9   Roger Maris
No. 10   Phil Rizzuto
No. 15   Thurman Munson
No. 16   Whitey Ford
No. 32   Elston Howard
No. 37   Casey Stengel

Four teams have yet to retire any numbers: Montreal and San Diego in the National League, and Seattle and Texas in the American League.

Gaining Honor

When Calvin Hill was growing up in Baltimore in the late 1950s, his hero was Alan Ameche, a rugged running back for the Baltimore Colts. Hill dreamed of following in his idol's footsteps, wearing Ameche's No. 35.

A powerful, long-striding runner, Hill never played for the Colts, but he did manage to make his numerical dream come true. He wore his chosen number as a high school player at the Riverdale Country School in the Bronx, New York, where he earned All-America honors.

At Yale, where he played college football, Hill had to settle for No. 30 because 35 was already taken. But he was No. 35 with the Dallas Cowboys from 1969 through 1974, with the Hawaiians of the World Football League in 1975, and for two seasons with the Washington Redskins and four with the Cleveland Browns.

Throughout his long career, Hill often described his No. 35 as being "very important" to him. So he was delighted to learn in 1986 that his number was being retired. It was not, to be sure, the Cowboys who were honoring him, nor the Hawaiians, the Redskins or the Browns. Instead, on October 25, 1986, No. 35 was officially retired by the Riverdale Country School.

On and Off

When third baseman Mike Pagliarulo joined the New York Yankees in 1984, he was handed uniform No. 45. That year and during the year that followed, the club kept changing Pagliarulo's number. He wore No. 6 for a while, then No. 12 and then No. 34. On opening day of the 1986 baseball season, Pagliarulo trotted out to his position at third base wearing No. 13.

Pagliarulo's number was changed more frequently, it was said, than Yankee owner George Steinbrenner changed managers. Pagliarulo's fans didn't like the treatment he was getting. One wrote to a New York newspaper to protest. "What will they do if they ever want to retire Pagliarulo's number," the fan asked, "pick it out of a hat?"

Preferred Number

Pro football's Karl Mecklenburg, a defensive back and later a linebacker for the Denver Broncos, like Red Grange wore No. 77. The reason that Mecklenburg was happy to wear the number had nothing to do with Grange. "My wife," Mecklenburg declared, "says my 7s are easy to pick out from the stands."

A City's Number

To sports fans in Los Angeles, No. 32 is special. For one thing, it was the number worn by Sandy Koufax, baseball's best pitcher of the 1960s, a Hall of Famer, whose record includes four strikeout titles and four no-hitters, one of them a perfect game. Koufax was the National League's Most Valuable Player in 1963, one of the years he helped to carry the Dodgers to victory in the World Series. He was also a major factor in 1966, when the Dodgers won the National League title.

Basketball star Earvin "Magic" Johnson of the Los Angeles Lakers was another No. 32. A dazzling ball handler, Johnson was a vital cog in the Lakers' success beginning with his rookie season of 1979–80. The team captured the championship of the National Basketball Association that season and again in 1981–82, 1984–85, 1986–87, and 1987–88.

Los Angeles had still another outstanding No. 32 in running back Marcus Allen of the Raiders. The winner of the Heisman Trophy as the nation's best college player in 1981, Allen rushed for a Super Bowl record of 191 yards in 1984, as the Raiders crushed the Washington Redskins, 38–9. The following season Allen led the NFL in ground gaining, with 1,759 yards.

Looking back on all of this, one fan came to this conclusion: "You can't have a championship in Los Angeles without a great No. 32."

A New Leaf

In baseball, the higher a player's number, the lower his sense of security. Someone who wears, say, a 49, 56 or a 62 on his back is usually a player on the brink, in danger of being shifted to a minor league team.

High numbers are distributed in the spring, when scores of young hopefuls join the veteran players at each team's training camp. Since the veterans have the numbers beginning with 1 (or 0 or 00) and continuing in sequence, the new-comers have to be satisfied with what remains. And what remains are numbers in the 50s, 60s and 70s. Occasionally even an 80 is seen.

How, then, does one explain the No. 72 worn by catcher Carlton Fisk? A star performer for the Boston Red Sox for a decade, Fisk became a free agent and signed with the Chicago White Sox in 1981. Fisk deserved a very low number, perhaps an 8, a number often worn by catchers.

It seems that Fisk felt that his switch from the Red Sox to the White Sox represented a real turnabout in his career. The change called for a new uniform number. In Boston, Fisk had always worn No. 27. So he turned it around, and the result was a number higher than that worn by any other major leaguer.

Compromise

When Rick Barry signed with the Houston
Rockets at the National Basketball Association
in 1978 after a long career with the Golden State
Warriors, he couldn't get the number he usually
wore—24. It was being worn by Moses Malone.
So Barry's solution was to wear No. 2 for home
games and No. 4 when the Rockets were playing
on the road.

A Name to Remember

In 1986, when the San Francisco Giants were honoring the team's all-time greats, the club management ran into a problem. It had to do with pitcher Christy Mathewson, who had won 372 games as a member of the New York Giants and one game for the Cincinnati Reds—373 games overall. Mathewson also won 11 games in World Series play. Mathewson retired in 1916 and was named to baseball's Hall of Fame twenty years later.

The usual way the Giants paid tribute to their outstanding players was to paint their numbers on the right field wall at Candlestick Park. These players had been so honored:

> Carl Hubbell   No. 11
> Juan Marichal   No. 27
> Willie Mays   No. 24
> Willie McCovey   No. 44
> Mel Ott   No. 4
> Bill Terry   No. 3

The problem with Mathewson was that he had no number to retire. He played in a time before uniforms carried numbers.

The Giants solved the problem by retiring Mathewson's *name*. Before an Old-Timers' game at Candlestick Park in 1986, a plaque with Mathewson's name on it went up on the wall.

"It's kind of unusual, retiring a name," said Pat Gallagher, a club vice president. "We talked for years about how to honor Mathewson. We felt this was the best way."

Someone then asked Gallagher what he would do if a young player ever showed up at spring training calling himself Christy Mathewson. Gallagher grinned. "We'd just have to come up with a new name for him," he said.

Superstars

When Julius Erving, perhaps the most exciting basketball player in the game's history, signed with the Philadelphia 76ers in 1976, he asked for jersey No. 32. That was the number he had worn with his previous team, the New York Nets. But Philadelphia's No. 32 was hanging from the rafters in the Spectrum, where the 76ers play their home games. It had been retired in tribute to Billy Cunningham, one of the team's all-time greats, who soon was to be named the Philadelphia coach.

Erving then decided to wear No. 6. For the rest of the 1970s and through most of the 1980s, Erving performed in spectacular fashion. He established No. 6 as his number. In 1988, the 76ers retired No. 6 in his honor.

Other players on other teams have helped to make their numbers well known in recent years. Here is a list of some of them:

Dale Murphy, *Atlanta Braves*   No. 6
George Brett, *Kansas City Royals*   No. 5
Dan Marino, *Miami Dolphins*   No. 13

Joe Montana, *San Francisco 49ers;* Bo Jackson, *Kansas City Royals;* Dwight Gooden, *New York Mets* No. 16

Michael Jordan, *Chicago Bulls;* Don Mattingly, *New York Yankees* No. 23

Earvin "Magic" Johnson, *Los Angeles Lakers;* Marcus Allen, *Los Angeles Raiders* No. 32

Larry Bird, *Boston Celtics;* Tony Dorsett, *Dallas Cowboys* No. 33

Wayne Gretzky, *Los Angeles Kings* No. 99

Leading the Way

Women players are still a rarity in most professional sports. Although they are well known in tennis and golf, women have yet to play professional baseball, football or hockey on a major league level.

In professional basketball, the barrier came down in 1986 when twenty-seven-year-old Nancy Lieberman signed a contract with the Springfield (Massachusetts) Fame of the United States Basketball League. A 5-foot-10 point guard, Lieberman had first become nationally known as a three-time All-America selection at Old Dominion College in Norfolk, Virginia.

Growing up in Brooklyn, where she was born, Lieberman played playground basketball on asphalt courts. Her idol was slick Walt Frazier, the New York Knicks superstar who later became a member of basketball's Hall of Fame. As the first woman to play professional basketball, Lieberman chose to wear Frazier's number—No. 10.

Tall Talk

Guard Rod Hundley, whose nickname was Hot Rod, joined the Minneapolis Lakers of the National Basketball Association in 1957 following a fine college career at West Virginia University. After the Lakers moved to Los Angeles in 1960, Hundley, a flashy playmaker, enjoyed his best seasons. One year he recorded 350 assists, the second highest total on the Laker team, and he averaged 11 points per game that season. After Hundley retired in 1963, he became successful in television as a sports broadcaster.

Hundley wore No. 33 as a pro player. He made reference to the number when he wrote his autobiography and titled it: *Clown: Number 33 in Your Program and Number 1 in Your Heart.*

While Hundley was always a solid performer, no one ever mistook him for a superstar. That's why he never failed to draw some smiles when he would announce, as he did frequently, "The Lakers are sure to retire my No. 33 as soon as that guy Kareem Abdul-Jabbar gets through using it."

Trivia Question III

Three notable major leaguers have had their uniform numbers retired by not one, but two teams. One of them is Casey Stengel. Stengel's No. 37 has been retired by both the New York Yankees and the New York Mets.

The second is Rod Carew, one of baseball's all-time great hitters. Carew's No. 29 has been retired by the California Angels and the Minnesota Twins.

Who is the third player?

Answer: see page 119

Number Shortage

When Jerry Sichting was traded from the Indiana Pacers to the Boston Celtics at the beginning of the 1985–86 basketball season, he asked for No. 14. But the number had been retired, he was told. It was now hanging amidst the rafters at the Boston Garden in honor of its last wearer, Bob Cousy, who had retired in 1963. Cousy has been called the best playmaker in basketball history.

Since No. 14 wasn't available, Sichting asked for No. 24. That was gone, too. No. 24 had been retired to honor Sam Jones, a sharp-shooting guard during Boston's glory years of the 1960s. Sichting eventually settled for No. 12.

As this suggests, the Boston Celtics have paid tribute to many players over the years. They have, in fact, retired more numbers than any other basketball team, fifteen of them. This isn't unusual when you consider that the Celtics, through 1986, had captured the National Basketball Association championship sixteen times. In other words, there are a great many Boston players who deserve to be honored.

Besides players, the Celtics have also paid tribute to Walter Brown, the founder of the team. The No. 1 jersey was retired to honor Brown. No. 2 was put in retirement to honor Arnold "Red" Auerbach, the team's former coach, later its general manager and, more recently, its president.

These are the fifteen numbers retired by the Celtics:

No.	1	Walter Brown
No.	2	Arnold "Red" Auerbach
No.	6	Bill Russell
No.	10	Jo Jo White
No.	14	Bob Cousy
No.	15	Tom Heinsohn
No.	16	Tom "Satch" Sanders
No.	17	John Havlicek
No.	18	Dave Cowens, Jim Loscutoff
No.	19	Don Nelson
No.	21	Bill Sharman
No.	22	Ed Macauley
No.	23	Frank Ramsey
No.	24	Sam Jones
No.	25	K. C. Jones

At the rate they're going, the Boston Celtics may one day run out of numbers. The players might have to start wearing letters on their backs instead.

Commercial Break

During the years that Andy Messersmith pitched for the Atlanta Braves, he wore No. 17. In 1976, the Braves decided it would be a good idea to stitch each player's nickname above his uniform number. Since Messersmith had no nickname, Ted Turner, owner of the Braves, declared that Andy should be nicknamed "Channel." The word was added to Andy's uniform above his number.

Turner's purpose was easy to understand. Besides the Braves, Turner also owned a television station in Atlanta, WTCH, Channel 17. Every time Andy put on his uniform, he became a walking billboard for the TV station.

Turner's joke attracted nationwide attention. Newspapers and TV stations showed Messersmith with "Channel 17" blazoned on his back. But National League President Chub Feeney did not laugh. He said what the Braves had done was a form of advertising, and advertising was not permitted on players' uniforms. He ordered the Braves to remove the word Channel. Messersmith went back to being just plain No. 17.

Super Number

Which team will win the next Super Bowl? If the past is any guide to the future, it will be the team whose quarterback wears No. 12.

Through the years, No. 12 wearers have accounted for nine Super Bowl triumphs. Winning quarterbacks who have worn No. 12 include Terry Bradshaw of the Pittsburgh Steelers, Bob Griese of the Miami Dolphins, Ken Stabler of the Oakland Raiders, and Joe Namath of the New York Jets.

Quarterback Jack Thompson of the Cincinnati Bengals was another No. 12 involved in a Super Bowl. He was a member of the Bengal squad that faced the San Francisco 49ers in the 1982 contest. But Thompson never got into the game. Maybe that's why the Bengals lost.

One of a Kind

Jim Otto, a center for the Oakland Raiders, was a man of many accomplishments. He started every game played by the Oakland team during the ten-year history of the American Football League (AFL). He was the AFL's one and only All-League center. He was voted into Pro Football's Hall of Fame in 1980, the very first year he was eligible for the honor.

Despite his many achievements, Otto is remembered more for the No. 00 he wore than anything else. (Otto was No. 50 during his rookie season. But always after, he was No. 00.)

"The guys on the team used to call me 'Ott,' " Otto once recalled. "That sounded like 'aught,' the word that means a cipher or zero. So the club decided that they would put a zero—a single 0—on my uniform."

At the time, however, a running back named Johnny Olszewski, who was nicknamed "Johnny O," was playing for the Washington Redskins of the NFL, and Olszewski was wearing an O. The Raiders didn't want Otto's number to be confused with Olszewski's letter, so they decided to give him two zeroes instead of one.

It was rare to see a uniform with No. 00 on it in those days, and Otto quickly became well known. But although the number earned him a certain distinction, he was often razzed by the fans because of it. "Otto, you're not nothing," one fan yelled, "you're *double* nothing!"

Another fan wanted to know whether the No. 00 represented Otto's I.Q.

Some of Otto's critics claimed the only reason he won All-League honors so many times was that he was so noticeable.

Otto shrugged off criticism. All the attention he got made up for it.

Otto retired from football in 1975. Originally from Wisconsin, he settled in Yuba City, California, where he became a successful businessman. He owned a restaurant and operated a land development company. He drives a car with a license plate that reads: I AM 00.

Department of Coincidences

In 1963, Hank Aaron, who wore No. 44, hit 44 home runs. That feat, however, didn't win him the National League's home run title that season; it merely earned him a tie. Willie McCovey hit 44 homers in 1963, too. And, of course, McCovey also wore No. 44.

Seeing Double

Twins who closely resemble each other and play the same sport have always presented a challenge to those who assign jersey numbers. Take the case of the Van Arsdale twins, Dick and Tom, whose names were well known to basketball fans of the 1960s and 1970s. Once, in a high school all-star game in Indianapolis, both were No. 1. But their first names were added to their backs to keep spectators from getting confused.

At the University of Indiana, Tom wore No. 25, while Dick was assigned No. 30.

Both wore No. 5 with their first pro teams, Dick with the New York Knicks, Tom with the Detroit Pistons.

Dick was traded to the Phoenix Suns in 1968, and later Tom joined him there. Since Dick already had No. 5, Tom had to be content with something else; he chose No. 4.

The 1980s brought another pair of twins onto the scene, the Doziers, Terry and Perry, basketball stars at the University of South Carolina.

The numbers they were assigned took no note of the fact that they were a unique pair. Terry wore No. 31, while Perry had No. 41.

Greater consideration went into selecting the uniform numbers of Larry and Harry Jones, football twins at the University of Kentucky during the 1960s. Larry wore No. 1A, Harry No. 1B.

Change of Heart

During the years that the Colts played in Baltimore, they were one of the winningest teams in pro football. They captured several conference and division titles and the National Football League championship twice, and appeared in two Super Bowls, winning Super Bowl V.

Between the years 1953 and 1976, the Colts never failed to produce at least one All-Pro player, and in one year, 1959, they boasted eight of them.

Seven Baltimore Colts are members of Pro Football's Hall of Fame. And their jersey numbers have been retired by the club. They are:

No. 19	Johnny Unitas
No. 22	Buddy Young
No. 24	Lenny Moore
No. 70	Art Donovan
No. 77	Jim Parker
No. 82	Raymond Berry
No. 89	Gino Marchetti

The Colts abandoned Baltimore after the 1983 season and moved to Indianapolis. There the team's earlier success caused a problem. The team's equipment manager began to run out of jersey numbers. It wasn't just because so many had been taken out of use. Another factor was that rosters were much bigger in the 1980s than they were in the 1960s: 49 players in 1984 compared with 37 in 1963. The equipment manager also had to contend with the league rule that required certain numbers for each position.

To help ease the number shortage, the Indianapolis Colts announced they planned to "unretire" the No. 82 once worn by Ray Berry and the No. 89 worn by Gino Marchetti.

That was a mistake. Baltimore fans of the Colts and former Colt players sent up a great storm of protest. "This is about as low as you can get," said Jim Parker, a former lineman with the team (and whose No. 77 had been retired). "It's like digging up a grave."

The next day, officials of the Indianapolis Colts changed their minds. It was announced that No. 82 and No. 89 would stay retired.

Baltimore fans and former players seemed satisfied and calmed down. But they're on their guard. If Indianapolis ever lays a hand on those retired numbers again, you'll hear their screams.

Hockey's Highest

Since there are relatively few players on a hockey team's roster, there's no need for high jersey numbers. Indeed, numbers beyond 35 are quite rare.

When you do see a high number, there's usually a good reason for it. For example, when Peter Klima, a forward for the Detroit Red Wings, picked out No. 85, he did it to commemorate 1985, the year he left his native Czechoslovakia to take up residence in the United States.

Mario Lemieux, a forward for the Pittsburgh Penguins, was greatly impressed by the awesome achievements of the great Wayne Gretzky, No. 99 for the Los Angeles Kings. Lemieux selected No. 66, Gretzky's number upside down. (The story of Gretzky and his No. 99 is told later in this book.)

Two of the most noted high numbers were worn by a pair of New York Rangers: Phil Esposito, No. 77, and Ken Hodge, No. 88. Both players were obtained by the Rangers from the Boston Bruins. Esposito had worn No. 7 in Boston; Hodge, No. 8. Since other players were wearing their numbers when they arrived in New York, Esposito and Hodge each settled on a double digit in order to wear the number he wanted.

Hometown Hero

Pitcher Bill Voiselle won 74 games in a major league career that began with the New York Giants in 1942 and ended with the Chicago Cubs in 1950. It was not a career that won Hall of Fame honors for Voiselle. In fact, he is usually remembered for his uniform number more than anything else.

In 1947, after he was traded from the Giants to the Boston Braves, Voiselle asked for and was given No. 96. Voiselle, you see, came from Ninety Six, South Carolina, and thought it would be nice to give his hometown some recognition.

Jinxed or Not?

Fear of the number thirteen—what is known as triskaidekaphobia—is quite common. The floor-button panels in the elevators of many tall buildings often don't show a number thirteen. The panels read, ". . . 10, 11, 12, 14, 15 . . ."

Commercial airlines refuse to have a Flight 13. And aboard commercial airliners, there are no seats or rows of seats with that number.

In professional sports, jersey No. 13 is usually avoided. Most teams won't give out a jersey with that number unless a player insists upon wearing it.

Take professional football, for instance. Of the approximately 1,400 players listed on the rosters of the National Football League's twenty-eight teams in 1989, only six players felt courageous enough to wear No. 13.

The number is rarely seen in either professional basketball or hockey. Some seasons, No. 13 is not worn at all; other years, one or two players wear it.

Hockey players who shun No. 13 may have

in mind what happened to Lars Lindgren, a defenseman with the Vancouver Canucks. Lindgren believed he was the victim of an injury jinx. To break the curse, Lindgren switched from a No. 3 jersey to a No. 13. His health improved, but during a game in November 1982 against the Edmonton Oilers, Lindgren shot the puck into his own net.

Despite such tales, there doesn't seem to be much solid evidence that wearing No. 13 is harmful to one's career. Baseball players frequently challenge the hex. In recent seasons, players who have worn the number have included: Ozzie Guillen, Chicago White Sox; Jeff Musselman, New York Mets; and Mike Pagliarulo, San Diego Padres.

Basketball's Wilt Chamberlain was another player who defied the No. 13 jinx. Chamberlain, who retired in 1972, still holds dozens of scoring records. These include the record for most points scored in a game (100) and most points scored in a season (4,029). In 1961–62, Chamberlain averaged 50.4 points per game, a record no other player has come close to. Chamberlain is one of the greatest players in basketball history, and

some people hail him as *the* greatest. For Wilt
Chamberlain No. 13 was anything but unlucky.

Into Triple Digits

If teams in baseball and football keep retiring numbers at the present rate, a shortage of two-digit numbers is sure to develop. Clubs will then be forced to issue numbers in the hundreds.

If you watch professional football on television, you may have noticed that the 99 barrier has already been broken. Several of the National Football League's on-the-field officials wear numbers in the hundreds.

There is, for example, the No. 101, worn by umpire Bob Boylston. Referee Dale Hamer wore No. 104, and line judge Joe Haynes No. 112. During the 1989–90 season, the highest number of all belonged to head linesman Tom White, who wore No. 123.

Most Popular

Of the seventy or so numbers retired by professional basketball teams over the years, No. 14 has been singled out more often than any other. Four wearers of No. 14 have been honored:

Bob Cousy, *Boston Celtics*
Jon McGlocklin, *Milwaukee Bucks*
Tom Meschery, *Golden State Warriors*
Oscar Robertson, *Sacramento Kings*

Why has No. 14 proven so popular? Maybe because it contains two "lucky" sevens,

Athletes Turned Sportscasters

Many of television's most noted sportscasters also had careers as athletes. Here's a rundown:

Frank Gifford, who announces Monday-night football games on ABC–TV, was a backfield star for the New York Giants during a part of the 1950s and 1960s. Gifford's number was 16.

Pat Summerall, a broadcaster on CBS–TV, was a Giant teammate of Gifford's in 1959 and 1960. Summerall, a kicker, also played for the Detroit Lions and Chicago Cardinals. He led the NFL in field goals in 1959. Summerall wore No. 88.

Ahmad Rashad, a member of the NBC–TV broadcasting team, wore No. 28 as a wide receiver for the Minnesota Vikings.

In baseball, there was Bob Uecker, an announcer for the Milwaukee Brewers and ABC–TV. Uecker, a catcher, had a lifetime batting average of .200. He billed himself as "The man who made mediocrity famous." Uecker wore No. 9.

Baseball broadcaster Joe Garagiola of NBC–

TV, also a catcher, played for a number of National League teams in the late 1940s and 1950s. He wore a different number with each team. One is special to him: No. 54. That was the number he was assigned after being traded in mid season from the Chicago Cubs to the New York Giants. The Giants promptly won the pennant and the World Series. The year of the trade: 1954.

Trivia Question IV

If 0 and 00 are the lowest numbers worn by professional athletes, what is the highest? It's 99, of course. (As of 1988, there were no players wearing three-digit numbers in professional sports.)

During the 1980s, about a dozen players in the National Football League wore No. 99. Can you name the player who became the most closely identified with the number?

Answer: see page 119

Sluggers' Numbers

Hank Aaron, with 755 home runs, the all-time leader in that department, wore No. 44 throughout almost all of his career, which covered 23 seasons. By the time he retired in 1976, Aaron and No. 44 were closely linked in the public's mind.

Willie McCovey, tenth on the all-time homer list, with 521 homers, also wore No. 44. McCovey, who played for the San Francisco Giants, was voted into baseball's Hall of Fame in 1986.

Reggie Jackson, a third well-known slugger, was yet another 44. Jackson, with 563 homers, is sixth on the all-time list.

Jackson didn't always wear No. 44. In the early years of his career, Reggie played for the Oakland A's and wore No. 9. He continued to wear that number until he was traded to the New York Yankees in 1976. There he found that No. 9 was being worn by third baseman Graig Nettles. It was then that Jackson chose No. 44, explaining he would be wearing it out of respect for Aaron and McCovey and their achievements. "I'm in very good company," Jackson said.

Here is a list of the top ten home-run hitters of all time, with the uniform number of each:

Player	Total Home Runs	Number
Hank Aaron	755	44
Babe Ruth	714	3
Willie Mays	660	24
Frank Robinson	586	20

Player	Total Home Runs	Number
Harmon Killebrew	573	3
Reggie Jackson	563	44
Mike Schmidt	548	20
Mickey Mantle	536	7
Jimmy Foxx	534	3
Ted Williams	521 ⎫	9
Willie McCovey	521 ⎭	44

365 FT.

Double Take

Danny Ainge wore No. 44 as a valued member of the Boston Celtics beginning in 1981. But earlier, when Ainge was considering a baseball career, he wore No. 2 as an infielder for the Toronto Blue Jays.

Ainge was one of a handful of players who competed in two sports, wearing a different number in each.

Gene Conley was another. Conley wore No. 22 as a pitcher for the Milwaukee Braves in the 1950s. But each fall when Conley turned to basketball, he became No. 17 for the Boston Celtics.

Dick Groat wore No. 24 as a shortstop for the Pittsburgh Pirates in the 1950s and early 1960s. As a basketball All-America at Duke, Groat wore No. 10.

Jackie Robinson, who broke baseball's color line in 1947, was skilled in several sports. As a second baseman for the Brooklyn Dodgers, Robinson made No. 42 famous. Before that, as a basketball star at UCLA, Robinson was No. 18.

Basketball's Best

Who is the greatest player in the history of professional basketball? Some people say Wilt Chamberlain, who holds dozens of the game's scoring records. Others point to Bill Russell, perhaps the best defensive player the game has known.

Russell himself had another opinion. "Kareem Abdul-Jabbar," Russell once said, "is the greatest player to play this game." Many people agreed. And it's no wonder. Abdul-Jabbar was, in effect, a scoring machine, pouring in more points than any other player in the history of the game. A member of the Los Angeles Lakers, Abdul-Jabbar was a major force in the team's many championship seasons during the 1980s. He retired in 1989.

Abdul-Jabbar wore No. 33. It has become the most celebrated number in basketball.

On January 20, 1986, not long before the Lakers were to play the Chicago Bulls in Chicago, someone stole Abdul-Jabbar's No. 33 jersey. For the game that night, Abdul-Jabbar wore No. 50.

Although he wasn't at his best, playing his second game in twenty-six hours, Abdul-Jabbar still finished with 27 points in the 31 minutes he played. The Lakers crushed the Bulls, 133–118.

In other words, the fans had no problem recognizing Kareem Abdul-Jabbar, even though he wasn't wearing his usual number. He was always the guy putting the ball in the basket more often than anyone else.

Unforgettable

In 1962, the year the team was founded, the New York Mets had a catcher named Clarence "Choo-Choo" Coleman. Choo-Choo had great trouble remembering names (and catching curve balls). Through his curious behavior, he became something of a legend.

When the Mets went to spring training in 1963, Charlie Neal was picked by the club to be Choo-Choo's roommate. Newspaper reporters went to Neal to get his reaction. "I'll bet he doesn't even remember me," said Neal, and he walked over to where Choo-Choo was seated. "Do you know who I am?" Neal asked. Choo-Choo looked Neal up and down. "Sure, I remember you," he said. "You're No. 4."

Nothing Numbers

Jerseys with either No. 0 or No. 00 used to be seen only once in a great while, and they attracted widespread attention. But in recent years more and more players have picked out No. 0 or No. 00, and fans are getting used to seeing them. In fact, during the 1986 baseball season, the Toronto Blue Jays had a pair of nothings for designated hitters: Al Oliver wore No. 0 and Cliff Johnson, No. 00.

In hockey, John Davidson, goalie for the New York Rangers, wore No. 00. Davidson was the first player in Ranger history to wear the number.

In professional basketball, Robert Parish of the Boston Celtics chose No. 00. "I had it in junior high school," he once explained, "and it has been with me since. I just like it."

Orlando Woolrich, a member of the New York Nets, preferred 0. But Woolrich wanted it made clear that his 0 was not a zero. It was really the letter O, the initial letter of his first name.

For one game during the 1987–88 season, the Los Angeles Lakers' James Worthy wore

No. 00. Worthy had a good reason for doing so—his usual jersey, No. 42, hadn't come back from the laundry.

Added Player

Through the years, teams in professional sports have honored hundreds of players, managers and coaches by retiring their numbers. The Boston Celtics of the National Basketball Association even honored the founder of the team, Walter Brown, in that manner, by retiring jersey No. 1.

One team, the Seattle Seahawks, retired a jersey as a tribute to their fans. At a pregame ceremony at the Kingdome on December 15, 1984, the Seahawks took jersey No. 12 out of use in recognition of the "tremendous support" the team had received from its fans.

Actually, "tremendous support" is something of an understatement. The uproar generated by the screaming Seattle fans in the closed-in Kingdome often makes it difficult for opposition quarterbacks to be clearly heard when calling signals. Broken plays frequently result.

Why was No. 12 chosen? "A football team is composed of eleven players," a spokesperson for the Seahawks explains. "But our fans give us one more player than other teams have,

a twelfth player." Rival quarterbacks might
agree.

The Heir

Right wing Gordie Howe was known as "Mister Hockey." During the sixteen years he skated for the Detroit Red Wings, from 1946 through 1971, Howe led the National Hockey League in scoring six times, and he was named the Most Valuable Player six times. "Gordie Howe plays a funny kind of game," an opposing player once said of him. "He doesn't let anyone else touch the puck."

Howe's two eldest sons, Mark and Marty, also played professional hockey. After their dad retired, many fans wondered which one of his sons would get Howe's famous No. 9.

Gordie himself made the decision. In doing so, he recalled that fans in rival arenas could often be cruel. Howe was no stranger to boos and ridicule.

Mark should get No. 9, Gordie determined. "You can't hurt Mark's feelings, whereas Marty is a thin-skinned guy," Gordie said. "I figure Mark is better able to handle the attention and abuse that goes with carrying my number."

Trivia Question V

What number was Babe Ruth wearing when he slammed home run number 60 on September 30, 1927?

Answer: see page 119

The One and Only

Wayne Gretzky of the Los Angeles Kings looms as hockey's greatest player. In 1989, he was awarded the Hart Trophy as the Most Valuable Player in the National Hockey League for the ninth time. In all of hockey history, no other player had won the league's MVP award more than six times. When Gretzky won the Art Ross Trophy in 1987 as hockey's scoring leader, it marked the seventh time he had captured that trophy.

Gretzky is notable for his distinctive jersey number, too—No. 99. Gretzky has worn No. 99 ever since he was a sixteen-year-old junior player at Sault Ste. Marie, Ontario, playing for the Sault Ste. Marie Greyhounds.

When Gretzky joined the Greyhounds, he wanted No. 9, which had been worn by Gordie Howe, one of hockey's all-time greats and Gretzky's boyhood hero. No. 9 had also been worn by Bobby Hull of the Chicago Black Hawks and Maurice Richard of the Montreal Canadiens, two other Hall of Famers.

But No. 9 was not available. Someone then suggested that Wayne wear two 9s instead of one. Wayne agreed. It wasn't very long before Gretzky had made No. 99 one of the best-known numbers in the sports world.

Dis-Honored

Tackle Ron Mix, 6 feet 4, 250 pounds, was always a solid performer for the San Diego Chargers of the old American Football League. (The AFL operated from 1960 through 1969 and then merged with the National Football League.) A rookie in 1960, Mix was named to the *Sporting News* All-Star team five times.

No one was surprised when, following Mix's retirement in 1969, the Chargers announced that they were retiring his uniform No. 74.

Mix did not play football in 1970. Then he decided he would like to give the game one more try. He signed with the Oakland Raiders in 1971. This move stunned his old team. Charger officials found it hard to believe that Mix would ever play for any other club but San Diego. They felt betrayed.

As a kind of punishment, the club decided to "un-retire" Mix's number. There was no pregame or half-time ceremony; they just did it. It marked the only time in sports history that an honored number has been made commonplace again.

One of a Kind

Robert Merrill, a noted performer for the Metropolitan Opera Association in New York, was often called upon to sing "The Star-Spangled Banner" before home games at Yankee Stadium. Sometimes he did so while wearing Yankee pinstripes. Merrill had a uniform number like no other: No. 1½.

More 24s

Most sports fans identify the great Willie Mays with No. 24, the number he wore throughout his long and distinguished career. But there are two other 24s, both of whom carved out important careers in government, who should be mentioned.

One was Bill Bradley, who was elected U.S. Senator from New Jersey in 1978 and reelected in 1984. Bradley wore No. 24 as a member of the New York Knicks from 1967 through 1977. An outstanding shooter, Bradley was a key contributor to the Knick championship teams of 1970 and 1973.

Byron R. White, nicknamed "Whizzer," who has served as an associate justice of the U.S. Supreme Court for more than a quarter of a century beginning in 1962, was another No. 24. White enjoyed a brief but notable career as a pro football running back. In 1938, when he played for the Pittsburgh Pirates (later to become the Steelers), White was the National Football League's leading rusher. White also wore

No. 24 as a college player at the University of
Colorado.

Answers to Trivia Questions

I, page 24: No. 5.

II, page 46: Edson Arantes do Nascimento, known throughout the world as Pelé.

III, page 73: Hank Aaron. Aaron's No. 44 has been retired by the Milwaukee Brewers and the Atlanta Braves.

IV, page 98: Mark Gastineau, former defensive end for the New York Jets.

V, page 111: He wasn't wearing any number! Baseball players didn't start wearing numbers on a regular basis until 1929.

Index of Player Names

121

122

124

About the Author

George Sullivan is the author of more than sixty books for young readers. Many of those books are about sports, but Mr. Sullivan has written books on a wide range of other topics as well, including witchcraft, nuclear submarines, computers, and photography. His interest in photography goes further than just writing about it—he takes the photographs that are used to illustrate some of his books.

Many of George Sullivan's books are meant for aspiring young athletes: QUARTERBACK, CENTER, PITCHER. ANY NUMBER CAN PLAY is for sports enthusiasts, whether or not they ever take the field.

About the Illustrator

John Caldwell is a nationally published car-
toonist whose work has appeared in magazines
and newspapers including *The Saturday Review, Esquire, National Lampoon,* and *The New
York Times.* A collection of his cartoons has
been published in a book titled, simply,
CALDWELL (1988).

Mr. Caldwell is also the author/illustrator of
EXCUSES, EXCUSES: *How to Get Out of Practi-
cally Anything* and has illustrated BEYOND A
REASONABLE DOUBT, by Melvyn Zerman.